animal talk

Other Books by John Lund

Animal Antics
Animal Wisdom
Life according to Maude

animal talk

a photo exposé by John Lund

written by Peter Stein

life lessons
from our
furry friends

**Andrews McMeel
Publishing**

Kansas City

animal talk

05 06 07 08 09 WKT 10 987654321

ISBN 13: 978-0-7407-5030-4
ISBN 10: 0-7407-5030-5
Library of Congress Control Number: 2004111411

Art Direction: Collette Carter
Design and Production: Heather Stewart Design

introduction

It's okay . . . you can admit. You talk to animals.
We may not go around bragging about it, but we all do
it. They're always there with an open ear, ready to
listen (even if they *are* a captive audience). Now those
beloved cats and dogs get a chance to talk back and
share just a bit of the wisdom they've kept hidden,
just beneath that playful canine bark or that
"Don't call me, I'll call you" feline attitude. *Animal Talk*
lets the cat (and the dog) out of the bag—our furry
friends have a thing or two to say about life and how to
live it. And it's no surprise: they spend a good deal of
their time watching us live ours! So sit back, relax, and
let them tell you what's on their minds . . . they'll give
you paws to reflect—and laugh too. Later, of course,
you can go back to doing most of the talking.

Life's a bowl of cherries.

Most of the time
it's sweet,
but once in a while
it's the pits.

The main thing is to relax.

Relax the mind,
the body, and of course
the ears.

And never underestimate
the power of a cheerful
attitude!
(A little coffee helps too.)

Most of all,
believe in yourself!
Believe in yourself!
Believe in yourself!

And believe in your hair!
Believe in your hair!
Believe in your hair

Stand tall
in the face of challenges,

13

lay low
when the storm hits,

and (yawn) nap
at every opportunity.

Tell yourself,
I think I can!
I think I can!
I think I can!

Unless of course
you think you can,
but you'd rather not.

Life throws new wrinkles
our way every day,

but it's nothing
you can't lick,

overcome,

**or tell just exactly
where to go.**

Still, sometimes stress
is inevitable...

you may just choose
to ignore it.

On the other hand,
you could lick it
into submission!

Then there are those
who like to stick
their neck out and
face it head on.

Still others prefer
to live in the la-la land
of denial and pretend stress
simply doesn't exist.

**Now *there's* a plan
I can live with!**

Speaking of stress,
don't you just hate it
when your job feels unfair
and your boss
is being mean...

and asks you to work
through your
mid-morning nap?

Sounds like *someone's* on a power trip.

If you MUST work,
at least try to do
what you love...

like being a professional
taster down at the
chocolate factory,

or the one they
practice on at
massage school.

Lots and lots and LOTS
of practice.

Another nice career choice:
Chief Researcher at the
Institute for Lazy People.

Wherever you go,
look life straight in the eye
and show it who's the boss.

**Unfortunately
this is not as effective
when you're having
a bad hair day.**

The point is, take charge.
Be the master of your
own destiny.

Helpful hint:
do this while being
cute and cuddly.

58

If you're not feeling
cute and cuddly,
then be calm and zen-like,
no matter what
comes your way.

That'll REALLY scare
the pants off everyone!

Let's face it—
we all have bad days,
when nothing goes
our way.

At times like these,
utilize the power of
positive thinking.

I *positively* hate my job!
I *positively* hate my clothes!
I *positively* hate my hair!

Actually,
it's much better to smile
through life's trivial things.

Most of it's just
fluff anyway.

Absolutely!

There are good spots to be found in *any situation!*

Most of all,
always remember —
there's no cooler cat than
the one in your mirror.

And that, my friend,
ain't no bull.